Couples ▪ *Couples* ▪ Paare

Photographs of Magnum Photos • *Photographies de Magnum Photos* • **Fotografien von Magnum Photos**

·TERRAIL·
PHOTO

Editor: Jean-Claude Dubost
Desk Editor: Caroline Broué
Graphic design: Véronique Rossi
Iconographic and artistic coordination at Magnum Photos:
Marie-Christine Biebuyck and Agnès Sire,
assisted by Philippe Devernay, Marta Campos and Inessa Quenum
English translation: Glenn Naumovitz
Photoengraving: Litho Service T. Zamboni, Verona

© FINEST SA / EDITIONS PIERRE TERRAIL, Paris, 1998
The Art Book Subsidiary of BAYARD PRESSE SA
Magnum Photos, Paris, 1998
ISBN 2-87939-195-4
English edition: © 1998
Publication number: 238
Printed in Italy.

Direction éditoriale : Jean-Claude Dubost
Assistante éditoriale : Caroline Broué
Conception et réalisation graphique : Véronique Rossi
Direction iconographique et artistique à Magnum Photos :
Marie-Christine Biebuyck et Agnès Sire,
assistées de Philippe Devernay, Marta Campos et Inessa Quenum
Traduction anglaise : Glenn Naumovitz
Traduction allemande : Inge Hanneforth
Photogravure : Litho Service T. Zamboni, Vérone

© FINEST SA / ÉDITIONS PIERRE TERRAIL, Paris, 1998
La filiale Livres d'art de BAYARD PRESSE SA
Magnum Photos, Paris, 1998
ISBN 2-87939-192-X
N° d'éditeur : 238
Dépôt légal : octobre 1998
Imprimé en Italie.

Verlegerische Leitung: Jean-Claude Dubost
Verantwortlich für die Ausgabe: Caroline Broué
Buchgestaltung: Véronique Rossi
Bildredaktion und gragische Gestaltung für Magnum Photos:
Marie-Christine Biebuyck, Agnès Sire;
Assistenten: Philippe Devernay, Marta Campos, Inessa Quenum
Deutsche Übersetzung: Inge Hanneforth
Farblithos: Litho Service T. Zamboni, Verona

© FINEST SA / EDITIONS PIERRE TERRAIL, Paris, 1998
Der Bereich Kunstbücher von BAYARD PRESSE SA
Magnum Photos, Paris, 1998
ISBN 2-87939-195-4
Deutsche Ausgabe: © 1998
Verlegernummer: 238
Printed in Italy.

They look and smile at each other, frolic, dance, hold hands, kiss, embrace, discuss, argue, break up and get back together again. Taken individually, each half of a couple has his or her own personal story. Together, they recount the adventure of the couple, a love relationship and the construction of a shared life. The mixture of their stories, as the photographer's eye sees them and as we perceive them, is what makes a theme like this one so rich. By seeking to capture the essentials of a scene in a 'decisive moment', Magnum photographers have managed to freeze stunning, loving moments in all their great variety.

What is most striking is the plurality of the couples presented. For example, the picture of the two Gypsies by Josef Koudelka at the beginning of the book does not have very much to do with the one by Elliott Erwitt showing two faces in love in the rear-view mirror of a car stopped on the seashore or the two young people Henri Cartier-Bresson caught by surprise in a Paris department store picking out a sofa for their future living-room. The Gypsies convey an image of a couple that could be called social. The dignified, bare-chested man is standing behind the woman with his hands on her shoulders and looking proudly at the lens. She is sitting, her thick, wrinkled hands crossed over her stomach. Her features are pronounced and the undefinable look on her face expresses strength and weariness at the same time. The couple photographed by Elliott Erwitt represents the romantic ideal of love. The woman's love and happiness are reflected in her smile and eyes. Lastly, the couple in the department store says it all about the desire to build a life together.

The diversity of the topic is matched by a multiplicity of looks, which in some cases can be ambiguous. At times the pictures contain several stories that can be interpreted on several different levels. For example, the photograph taken by Ian Berry in South Africa in 1979 has two meanings. It can either just show a couple on a beach, or have political and social significance. In fact, the picture went round the world as an image against apartheid. On the left, a couple holding hands can be seen walking on the beach from behind. On the right, two men seem to be playing and running after them. The interpretation could stop there. But the couple is white, and the two men are black. Furthermore, the picture is constructed in such a way that everything separates the two pairs of protagonists, who occupy a demarcated space. The line dividing them reflects racial discrimination.

Complementary or antagonistic, these photographs depict life's joys and contradictions, emphasizing the richness of the situations captured and the possible ways of interpreting them. From the intimacy suggested by an embrace to the stolen kiss and the intense look, from the new couple to the settled household, the continuously changing image of the couple is what can be appreciated here.

Jean-Claude Dubost

Is se regardent, se sourient, jouent, dansent, se tiennent par la main, s'embrassent, s'enlacent, discutent, se disputent, s'unissent... Ce sont des couples qui, pris séparément, évoquent chacun une histoire personnelle, la leur, et qui, ensemble, racontent l'aventure du couple, relation amoureuse et construction d'une vie commune. C'est ce mélange de leurs histoires, du regard du photographe et de notre perception qui crée la richesse d'un tel thème. En cherchant à capter l'essentiel d'une scène dans un « instant décisif », les photographes de Magnum ont su retenir des instants amoureux saisissants qu'ils nous restituent dans leur plus grande variété.

En effet, ce qui frappe avant tout, c'est la pluralité des figures du couple proposées : la photo des deux Gitans vus par Josef Koudelka au début du livre, par exemple, a peu de chose à voir avec celle d'Elliott Erwitt montrant deux visages amoureux dans le rétroviseur d'une voiture arrêtée au bord de la mer, ou encore avec la photo de ces jeunes gens surpris par Henri Cartier-Bresson dans un grand magasin à Paris en train de choisir le canapé de leur futur salon. Les premiers donnent une image du couple que l'on peut qualifier de sociale. L'homme, debout derrière la femme, digne, le torse nu, pose ses mains sur les épaules de celle-ci et regarde fièrement l'objectif. Elle, assise devant nous, les mains épaisses et ridées croisées sur son ventre, les traits marqués, dégage par la profondeur de son regard une expression indéfinissable de force et de fatigue à la fois. Les deuxièmes représentent plutôt l'idée romantique du couple. Dans les yeux et le sourire de la femme se reflètent son amour et son bonheur. Enfin, les derniers disent toute la volonté de construction d'une vie commune.

Cette diversité du sujet se double d'une multiplicité de points de vue, qui peut devenir ambiguïté dans certains cas. Car les photos contiennent parfois plusieurs histoires qui permettent plusieurs niveaux de lecture. Ainsi, cette photo de Ian Berry prise en Afrique du Sud en 1979 est à double sens : elle peut soit juste montrer un couple sur une plage, soit traduire un fait politique et social, en l'occurrence l'apartheid. On y voit, à gauche, un couple de dos, main dans la main, marchant sur la plage, et, à droite, deux hommes semblant jouer et se courir après. On pourrait s'arrêter là dans la lecture de l'image. Mais les premiers sont blancs, les deuxièmes noirs. En outre, la photo est construite de telle sorte que tout les divise : les protagonistes occupent deux par deux un espace délimité ; la ligne de séparation graphique reflète la discrimination raciale.

Complémentaires ou antagonistes, ces photos dépeignent les trésors et les contradictions de la vie, soulignant ainsi la richesse des situations saisies et des lectures possibles. De la complicité suggérée à l'étreinte, du baiser volé au regard intense, du couple naissant au ménage installé, c'est une image sans cesse renouvelée du couple que l'on peut apprécier ici.

Jean-Claude Dubost

Sie schauen und lächeln sich an, spielen, tanzen, halten sich an der Hand, küssen und umarmen sich, reden und streiten miteinander und schließen den Bund fürs Leben ... Es sind Paare, die, jedes für sich, ihre eigene Geschichte haben und die gemeinsam das Abenteuer dieser Gemeinschaft erzählen, das Verliebtsein, das Zusammenleben. Die Vielfältigkeit ihrer Geschichten, der Blick des Fotografen und unsere Betrachtungsweise machen das eigentliche Interesse eines solchen Thema aus. Dadurch, daß die Fotografen von Magnum das Essentielle eines "entscheidenden Augenblicks" festzuhalten suchen, bieten sie uns besonders anschauliche und höchst verschiedenartige Bilder von Verliebten.

Die Unterschiedlichkeit der hier abgelichteten Paare überrascht besonders: Das Foto der beiden von Josef Koudelka aufgenommenen Zigeuner gleich am Anfang hat beispielsweise wenig zu tun mit dem von Elliott Erwitt, auf dem im Rückspiegel eines am Meer parkenden Autos die Gesichter zweier Verliebter zu sehen sind, oder das Foto des jungen, von Henri Cartier-Bresson in einem Pariser Kaufhaus überraschten Paares beim Aussuchen eines Sofas für ihr zukünftiges Heim. Die ersten geben ein Bild ab, das man als sozial bezeichnen kann. Der hinter der Frau stehende Mann mit würdigem Gesichtsausdruck und nacktem Oberkörper hat die Hände auf die Schultern seiner Frau gelegt und schaut stolz ins Objektiv. Sie, sitzend, mit klobigen, faltigen, über dem Bauch gekreuzten Händen und scharfen Gesichtszügen, drückt etwas Undefinierbares voller Stärke und Müdigkeit zugleich aus. Das zweite Paar veranschaulicht eher die romantische Idee des Paares. Der Blick und das Lächeln der Frau geben Glück und Liebe zu erkennen. Und beim dritten Paar errät man den Wunsch nach dem Aufbau eines gemeinsamen Lebens.

Dieses Thema kann selbstverständlich auf ganz unterschiedliche Art betrachtet werden. Denn die Fotos enthalten oft mehrere Geschichten, die zahlreiche Interpretationen zulassen. So das 1979 in Südafrika von Ian Berry aufgenommene Foto: Es zeigt ein Paar am Strand, kann aber auch einen sozialen oder politischen Hintergrund haben. In jedem Fall ging es um die ganze Welt, um die Apartheid anzuprangern. Das Foto hält links ein auf dem Strand gehendes Paar von hinten fest, Hand in Hand, und rechts zwei Männer, die zu spielen und hintereinander herzulaufen scheinen. Das sieht man zumindest auf den ersten Blick. Die ersten sind jedoch weiß, die anderen schwarz. Außerdem ist das Foto derart aufgebaut, daß alles sie voneinander trennt: Die Protagonisten füllen den begrenzten Raum paarweise aus; die grafische Trennlinie spiegelt die Rassendiskriminierung wider.

Diese sich ergänzenden oder gegensätzlichen Fotos veranschaulichen die Schätze und Widersprüche des Lebens: festgehaltene Momente, die ganz unterschiedliche Betrachtungsweisen erlauben. Angefangen vom geheimen Einverständnis bis zur Umarmung, vom geraubten Kuß bis zum tiefen Blick, von einer Frau und einem Mann, die sich gerade begegnen, bis zur ehelichen Gemeinschaft zeigt dieser Fotoband ein immer wieder anderes Bild des Paares.

Jean-Claude Dubost

René Burri, Brazil, *Brésil, Brasilien,* 1960. **7**

8 | Elliott Erwitt, France, *France, Frankreich,* 1989.

Peter Marlow, Great Britain, *Grande-Bretagne*, Großbritannien, 1997. **9**

Guy Le Querrec, France, *France,* Frankreich, 1981.

Peter Marlow, England, *Angleterre,* England, 1982.

Martine Franck, Spain, *Espagne,* Spanien, 1993. | **13**

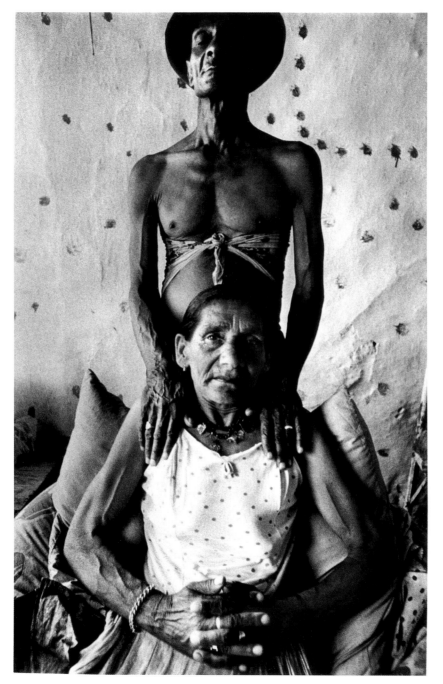

Josef Koudelka, Czechoslovakia, *Tchécoslovaquie,* Tschechoslowakei, 1967. | **15**

Elliott Erwitt, USA, *États-Unis*, USA, 1955. **17**

Bruce Davidson, USA, *États-Unis,* USA, 1959. **19**

Guy Le Querrec, GRD, *RDA*, DDR, 1989.

Henri Cartier-Bresson, USA, *États-Unis,* USA, 1971. **21**

Ian Berry, South Africa, *Afrique du Sud,* Südafrika, 1979. **23**

Raymond Depardon, USA, *États-Unis,* USA, 1981. **25**

Miguel Rio Branco, Brazil, *Brésil,* Brasilien, 1993.

David Hurn, Italy, *Italie,* Italien, 1963. **29**

Burt Glinn, USA, *États-Unis,* USA, 1961.

Richard Kalvar, USA, *États-Unis,* USA, 1970.

Harry Gruyaert, Belgium, *Belgique,* Belgien, 1975. **33**

Guy Le Querrec, France, *France,* Frankreich, 1990.

Ian Berry, South Africa, *Afrique du Sud,* Südafrika, 1961. | **35**

Ian Berry, England, *Angleterre,* England, 1964.

40 René Burri, South Korea, *Corée du Sud,* Südkorea, 1961.

Sergio Larrain, Chile, *Chili,* Chile, 1963. **41**

| Burt Glinn, USA, *États-Unis,* USA, 1955.

Eve Arnold, Cuba, *Cuba,* Cuba, 1954. **45**

Bruno Barbey, Italy, *Italie,* Italien, 1966. **47**

Dennis Stock, USA, *États-Unis,* USA, 1952. **49**

Henri Cartier-Bresson, France, *France,* Frankreich, 1968.

Martin Parr, United Kingdom, *Royaume-Uni,* Großbritannien, 1990. **51**

Larry Towell, Mexico, *Mexique,* Mexiko, 1992.

Dennis Stock, USA, *États-Unis,* USA, 1958. **55**

| Elliott Erwitt, France, *France, Frankreich,* 1975.

Page 7: Rio de Janeiro, Brazil.
René Burri, 1960.
Page 7 : *Rio de Janeiro, Brésil.*
René Burri, 1960.
Seite 7: Rio de Janeiro, Brasilien.
René Burri, 1960.

Page 8: Louvre Pyramid, Paris, France.
Elliott Erwitt, 1989.
Page 8 : *Pyramide du Louvre, Paris, France.*
Elliott Erwitt, 1989.
Seite 8: Pyramide des Louvre, Paris, Frankreich.
Elliott Erwitt, 1989.

Page 9: The Isle of Sheppey, Great Britain.
Peter Marlow, 1997.
Page 9 : *L'île de Sheppey, Grande-Bretagne.*
Peter Marlow, 1997.
Seite 9: Die Insel Sheppey, Großbritannien.
Peter Marlow, 1997.

Pages 10-11: Car rally at the senior management business school in Neuilly-sur-Seine, France.
Guy Le Querrec, 1981.
Pages 10-11 : *Rallye automobile de l'école des cadres de Neuilly-sur-Seine, France.*
Guy Le Querrec, 1981.
Seite 10-11: Rallye der Ecole des Cadres von Neuilly-sur-Seine, Frankreich.
Guy Le Querrec, 1981.

Page 12: London, England.
Peter Marlow, 1982.
Page 12 : *Londres, Angleterre.*
Peter Marlow, 1982.
Seite 12: London, England.

Peter Marlow, 1982.

Page 13: Retiro Park, Madrid, Spain.
Martine Franck, 1993.
Page 13 : *Parc de Retiro, Madrid, Espagne.*
Martine Franck, 1993.
Seite 13: Retiro-Park, Madrid, Spanien.
Martine Franck, 1993.

Page 15: Gypsies in Zehra, Czechoslovakia.
Josef Koudelka, 1967.
Page 15 : *Gitans à Zehra, Tchécoslovaquie.*
Josef Koudelka, 1967.
Seite 15: Zigeuner in Zehra, Tschechoslowakei.
Josef Koudelka, 1967.

Pages 16-17: California, USA.
Elliott Erwitt, 1955.
Pages 16-17 : *Californie, États-Unis.*
Elliott Erwitt, 1955.
Seite 16-17: Kalifornien, USA.
Elliott Erwitt, 1955.

Page 18: Brooklyn, New York, USA.
Bruce Davidson, 1959.
Page 18 : *Brooklyn, New York, États-Unis.*
Bruce Davidson, 1959.
Seite 18: Brooklyn, New York, USA.
Bruce Davidson, 1959.

Page 19: New York City, USA.
Bruce Davidson, 1959.
Page 19 : *New York, États-Unis.*
Bruce Davidson, 1959.
Seite 19: New York, USA.
Bruce Davidson, 1959.

Page 20: On the Berlin Wall,

Brandenburg Gate, GDR.
Guy Le Querrec, December 31, 1989.
Page 20 : *Sur le mur de Berlin, porte de Brandenbourg, RDA.*
Guy Le Querrec, 31 décembre 1989.
Seite 20: An der Berliner Mauer, Brandenburger Tor, DDR.
Guy Le Querrec, 31. Dezember 1989.

Page 21: Colorado, Aspen, USA. July 4th, Independence Day.
Henri Cartier-Bresson, 1971.
Page 21 : *Colorado, Aspen, États-Unis. 4 juillet, fête de l'Indépendance.*
Henri Cartier-Bresson, 1971.
Seite 21: Colorado, Aspen, USA. 4. Juli, Unabhängigkeitstag.
Henri Cartier-Bresson, 1971.

Page 23: Cape Town, South Africa.
Ian Berry, 1979.
Page 23 : *Le Cap, Afrique du Sud.*
Ian Berry, 1979.
Seite 23: Kapstadt, Südafrika.
Ian Berry, 1979.

Pages 24-25: On the Staten Island ferry. Manhattan, New York, USA.
Raymond Depardon, 1981.
Pages 24-25 : *Sur le ferry menant à Staten Island. Manhattan, New York, États-Unis.*
Raymond Depardon, 1981.
Seite 24-25: Auf der Fähre nach Staten Island. Manhattan, New York, USA.

Raymond Depardon, 1981.

Page 26: Guanabara Bay, Brazil.
Miguel Rio Branco, 1993.
Page 26 : *Baie de Guanabara, Brésil.*
Miguel Rio Branco, 1993.
Seite 26: Bucht von Guanabara, Brasilien.
Miguel Rio Branco, 1993.

Page 27: Under the 'betting booths' of the Deauville race track, France.
Leonard Freed, 1964.
Page 27 : *Sous les cabines des paris de l'hippodrome de Deauville, France.*
Leonard Freed, 1964.
Seite 27: Unter den „Wettkabinen" der Pferderennbahn von Deauville, Frankreich.
Leonard Freed, 1964.

Page 28: Allepey, Kerala, India.
Carl De Keyzer, 1987.
Page 28 : *Allepey, Kerala, Inde.*
Carl De Keyzer, 1987.
Seite 28: Allepey, Kerala, Indien.
Carl De Keyzer, 1987.

Page 29: At the local beach near Lecce, Italy.
David Hurn, 1963.
Page 29 : *Sur la plage près de Lecce, Italie.*
David Hurn, 1963.
Seite 29: Auf dem Strand bei Lecce, Italien.
David Hurn, 1963.

Pages 30-31: At a drive-in, watching a scene from the movie *Exodus*. USA.

Burt Glinn, 1961.
Pages 30-31 : *Cinéma en plein air, devant une scène du film* Exodus. *États-Unis. Burt Glinn, 1961.*
Seite 30-31: Eine in einem Drive-in betrachtete Szene des Films *Exodus*. USA. Burt Glinn, 1961.

■ **Page 32:** In front of the Museum of Modern Art, New York City, USA. Richard Kalvar, 1970.
Page 32 : *Devant le musée d'Art moderne, New York, États-Unis. Richard Kalvar, 1970.*
Seite 32: Vor dem Museum of Modern Art, New York City, USA. Richard Kalvar, 1970.

■ **Page 33:** Between Ostende and Brussels, Belgium. Harry Gruyaert, 1975.
Page 33 : *Entre Ostende et Bruxelles, Belgique. Harry Gruyaert, 1975.*
Seite 33: Zwischen Ostende und Brüssel, Belgien. Harry Gruyaert, 1975.

■ **Page 34:** Wedding in the village of Îlet à Bourse, Mafate circus, the Réunion. Guy Le Querrec, 1990.
Page 34 : *Mariage dans le village de Îlet à Bourse, cirque de Mafate, la Réunion. Guy Le Querrec, 1990.*
Seite 34: Hochzeit im Dorf Îlet à Bourse, Talkessel von Mafate, Réunion. Guy Le Querrec, 1990.

■ **Page 35:** A multiracial café in Johannesburg, South Africa. Ian Berry, 1961.

Page 35 : *Un café multiracial à Johannesburg, Afrique du Sud. Ian Berry, 1961.*
Seite 35: Ein Multi-Rassen-Café in Johannesburg, Südafrika. Ian Berry, 1961.

■ **Page 36:** Aids candlelight memorial in Castro Street, San Francisco, USA. Paul Fusco, 1991.
Page 36 : *Manifestation aux chandelles en hommage aux victimes du sida, Castro Street, San Francisco, États-Unis. Paul Fusco, 1991.*
Seite 36: Kerzen-Demonstration zum Gedenken der Aids-Opfer, Castro Street, San Francisco, USA. Paul Fusco, 1991.

■ **Page 37:** New Year at Trafalgar Square, London, England. Ian Berry, 1964.
Page 37 : *Le 31 décembre à Trafalgar Square, Londres, Angleterre. Ian Berry, 1964.*
Seite 37: Neujahr am Trafalgar Square, London, England. Ian Berry, 1964.

■ **Page 38:** Tynemouth Priory, Tyne and Wear, England. Martine Franck, 1978.
Page 38 : *Prieuré de Tynemouth, Tyne and Wear, Angleterre. Martine Franck, 1978.*
Seite 38: Tynemouth Priory, England. Martine Franck, 1978.

■ **Page 39:** Italy. Henri Cartier-Bresson, 1933.

Page 39 : *Italie. Henri Cartier-Bresson, 1933.*
Seite 39: Italien. Henri Cartier-Bresson, 1933.

■ **Page 40:** Yon Sul Gol village, South Korea. René Burri, 1961.
Page 40 : *Village de Yon Sul Gol, Corée du Sud. René Burri, 1961.*
Seite 40: Das Dorf Yon Sul Gol, Südkorea. René Burri, 1961.

■ **Page 41:** Valparaíso, Chile. Sergio Larrain, 1963.
Page 41 : *Valparaíso, Chili. Sergio Larrain, 1963.*
Seite 41: Valparaíso, Chile. Sergio Larrain, 1963.

■ **Pages 42-43:** Leningrad, USSR. Carl De Keyzer, 1989.
Pages 42-43 : *Leningrad, URSS. Carl De Keyzer, 1989.*
Seite 42-43: Leningrad, UdSSR. Carl De Keyzer, 1989.

■ **Page 44:** Hospital, USA. Burt Glinn, 1955.
Page 44 : *Hôpital, États-Unis. Burt Glinn, 1955.*
Seite 44: Krankenhaus, USA. Burt Glinn, 1955.

■ **Page 45:** Bahia Honda, Cuba. Eve Arnold, 1954.
Page 45 : *Bahia Honda, Cuba. Eve Arnold, 1954.*
Seite 45: Bahia Honda, Kuba. Eve Arnold, 1954.

■ **Page 47:** Palermo, Sicily, Italy. Bruno Barbey, 1966.
Page 47 : *Palerme, Sicile,*

Italie. Bruno Barbey, 1966.
Seite 47: Palermo, Sizilien, Italien. Bruno Barbey, 1966.

■ **Page 48:** Jack Paar and his wife lying in bed with dachshund and watching the Jack Paar Show taped earlier in the evening. USA. Cornell Capa, 1959.
Page 48 : *Jack Paar, sa femme et leur teckel sur leur lit en train de regarder le Jack Paar Show enregistré plus tôt dans la soirée. États-Unis. Cornell Capa, 1959.*
Seite 48: Jack Paar und seine Frau liegen mit ihrem Dackel auf dem Bett und sehen sich die früher am Abend aufgenommene Jack-Paar-Show an. USA. Cornell Capa, 1959.

■ **Page 49:** 'Love story'. Hartford, Connecticut, USA. Dennis Stock, 1952.
Page 49 : *« Love story ». Hartford, Connecticut, États-Unis. Dennis Stock, 1952.*
Seite 49: „Love story". Hartford, Connecticut, USA. Dennis Stock, 1952.

■ **Page 50:** Galeries Lafayette department store, Paris, France. Henri Cartier-Bresson, 1968.
Page 50 : *Aux Galeries Lafayette, Paris, France. Henri Cartier-Bresson, 1968.*
Seite 50: Galeries Lafayette, Paris, Frankreich. Henri Cartier-Bresson, 1968.

■ **Page 51:** 'Signs of time, a

portrait of a nation's taste'.
Based on the BBC television
series, it surveys contemporary
perceptions of good and bad
taste. United Kingdom.
Martin Parr, 1990.
Page 51 : *« Signes du temps,
un portrait des goûts d'une
nation ». Inventaire des
perceptions contemporaines du
bon et du mauvais goût basé
sur une série télévisée de la
BBC. Royaume-Uni.*
Martin Parr, 1990.
Seite 51: „Zeichen der Zeit,
ein Porträt über den
Geschmack einer Nation".
Basierend auf der
Fernsehserie der BBC,
untersucht es die damalige
Auffassung von gutem und
schlechtem Geschmack.
Großbritannien.
Martin Parr, 1990.

■ **Pages 52-53:** On the waggon
of oats. Mennonite community.
Campo 44, Cuautemoc,
Chihuahua, Mexico.
Larry Towell, 1992.
Pages 52-53 : *Sur la charette
d'avoine. Communauté
mennonite. Campo 44,
Cuautemoc, Chihuahua,
Mexique.*
Larry Towell, 1992.
Seite 52-53: Auf dem
Haferwagen. Mennoniten-
Gemeinschaft. Campo 44,
Cuautemoc, Chihuahua,
Mexiko.
Larry Towell, 1992.

■ **Page 54:** 'Prom Night',
Atlanta, Georgia, USA.
Eli Reed, 1995.
Page 54 : *« Prom Night »
(nuit de bal célébrant la fin des
études au lycée), Atlanta,*

Géorgie, États-Unis.
Eli Reed, 1995.
Seite 54: „Prom Night"
(Abiturfest), Atlanta, Georgia,
USA.
Eli Reed, 1995.

■ **Page 55:** The Savoy jazz club,
New York, USA.
Dennis Stock, 1958.
Page 55 : *Boîte de jazz Le
Savoy, New York, États-Unis.*
Dennis Stock, 1958.
Seite 55: Der Jazzclub Savoy,
New York, USA.
Dennis Stock, 1958.

■ **Pages 56-57:** Sunday on the
Marne river, France.
Henri Cartier-Bresson, 1938.
Pages 56-57 : *Un dimanche
au bord de la Marne, France.*
Henri Cartier-Bresson, 1938.
Seite 56-57: Ein Sonntag an
der Marne, Frankreich.
Henri Cartier-Bresson, 1938.

■ **Pages 58 and 59:** The
Croisette in Cannes, Côte
d'Azur, France.
Elliott Erwitt, 1975.
Pages 58 et 59 : *La Croisette
à Cannes, Côte d'Azur, France.*
Elliott Erwitt, 1975.
Seiten 58 und 59: Die
Croisette in Cannes, Côte
d'Azur, Frankreich.
Elliott Erwitt, 1975.